SECRET TIPS: HOW TO SURVIVE & HELP THE ALCOHOLIC YOU LOVE

By Randy Young
Author/Illustrator

DEDICATION

"To My Dear Family and Friends who encouraged and supported me throughout the writing of this book."

INTRODUCTION

Nearly every person who reads this book has had more than a passing acquaintance with an alcoholic. I refer to the alcoholic throughout this book in the male gender because that is the more common scenario. Please feel free to substitute gender as you read if you are one of many husbands who have a wife who suffers from alcoholism. Many of you have been deeply affected by an alcoholic; in fact, there are more people affected by alcoholics than there are alcoholics. I am no exception. From my circle of friends to the hundreds of alcoholics I've had the privilege of working with over three decades of professional practice, I am grateful for all I have learned. When I worked on a bridge construction crew I encountered persons who struggled with alcoholism. I would not forget the people I met, or the experiences. Eventually I found myself working at a state mental health institute which further introduced me to individuals struggling with alcoholism. As I pursued my academic goals, I continued to work at the mental health institute, working first in nursing, then social work, and eventually psychology and administration. Each discipline gave me a different perspective of the alcoholic, their family and associates, and what worked and didn't work to help them achieve sobriety.

While continuously working to improve the quality of the traditional alcohol treatment program at the Institute, I also helped design specialized programs for alcoholics. One of these programs was for women in recovery; another program was a long-term residential program for chronic male alcoholics; a program close to my heart was the family program I helped develop and implement. I had a chance to see the impact alcoholism had on the parents, spouses, children and friends who participated in the family program. Many of these significant others were at wit's end, with no idea of what to do next or where to go for help. Many of these folks had enabled the alcoholic only to see matters get worse. Threats and promises were to no avail. Not only was the life of the alcoholic spiraling out of control, so were the lives of those closest to the alcoholic.

In this book, I offer *secret* tips to help the alcoholic and persons closest to the alcoholic. Why do I refer to these tips as secret? It is not because the information is completely unknown. Indeed, it is not! Many recovering alcoholics and family members will be familiar with the points I make in this book. I refer to these tips as *secret* because too many family members and alcoholics, who *need the information the most,* don't have the information; it is *secret* to them. They don't know what to do or where to get help. I don't make any pretense of having all the answers, but I do believe the information I've gleaned from many persons and experiences over several years may help provide some guidance as to what to do and where to get additional help. Thank you for letting me share with you what has been shared with me.

Randy Young, Author

TABLE OF CONTENTS

TIP # 1: YOUR MAIN FOCUS MUST BE ON YOU, *NOT* THE ALCOHOLIC!

Confused? Wondering why the focus should start with you and not the alcoholic? Let me explain why. First of all, *the only person you can truly change is you*. You have the control and ability to learn new information, and to change how you think, feel and act. Chances are you have already tried nearly everything you can think of to get the alcoholic to stop drinking. You may have made excuses for the alcoholic's drinking behavior, taken over responsibilities, tried to bargain with the alcoholic, threatened, bailed him out of trouble, and pleaded and bargained to no avail. These failed attempts to change the alcoholic are further evidence that your focus has been on the wrong person.

It is important to accept that *you cannot change or control the alcoholic.* Therefore, it is futile to focus your energy and resources on that which you cannot change. Do not second guess this fact. Later on we will discuss how you may help or influence the alcoholic, but you must realize that you *never* have control of whether an alcoholic decides to work towards sobriety. In fact, many practicing alcoholics haven't reached that point in their lives where they are ready to make the decision to stay sober. This fact may put the alcoholic at odds with you if you have reached that point where you desperately want your alcoholic to stop drinking. Because he doesn't want to stop drinking, he may break promises, lie, manipulate and try to manage his life so he can keep drinking while trying to keep you marginally satisfied with the status quo. Meanwhile, every effort you make to get him to stop drinking fails.

Let's say the alcoholic has reached a decision to change. Does that take the focus off you? **No**.

Alcoholics who want to stay sober may not know how. They may need lots of ongoing help and it is likely to require several attempts interspersed with relapses before they finally achieve lasting sobriety. The alcoholic who decides to stay sober owns that decision and is responsible for the ongoing actions it takes to remain sober. *You are not responsible for the alcoholic's decision to stay sober, what he does to stay sober or whether he relapses. The alcoholic is the one in control of his sobriety.* However, *by focusing on making positive changes in your thinking, feelings and actions, you can present a positive frame of reference for comparison and avoid adding to the problem through self-defeating efforts to control that which you cannot control.* Finally, there is an even more important reason for focusing on self.

You must focus on self because *you are responsible for learning what you need to learn but don't know*. This may include where to get help, what changes you need to make, and who can help you. Many of these changes you are responsible for will include changes in your attitudes, feelings, actions, your schedule, who you spend time with, and other aspects of your life. These are changes you are responsible for and that will take time. Relapses are likely. *Resistance from self and others to change must also be expected*. In the following chapter, I will help you begin this journey. So, now it's time to get busy!

TIP # 2: LEARN WHAT YOU DON'T KNOW!

Now that I've impressed upon you the idea that the focus for change needs to start with you, you may be feeling even more overwhelmed than before. Don't worry, you are now on the right track and there is help available. Admitting and then accepting that you don't have the answers and that you do need help actually puts you in a much better position than believing that you can change the alcoholic. *What you don't know can hurt you and others!* For example, failed attempts to control the alcoholic you love can have a negative impact on your emotional and physical health, your relationship with the alcoholic, your social life, and the lives of your children. In addition, failed attempts to control the alcoholic may unintentionally reinforce the alcoholic's self-defeating behavior. So…what is it you don't know that you need to know?

To start with, you've already learned a couple of the facts you needed to know – *that you can't control the alcoholic and that the focus for change needs to be on you.* You also need to learn everything you can about alcoholism from its definition to its symptoms and far-reaching effects on others in our families and society. *Alcoholism can be defined as a pattern of drinking that results in negative consequences or problems for the person consuming the alcohol or those individuals close to the person using the alcohol.* There are many definitions of alcoholism and sources of information about alcoholism. One of best sources for information about alcoholism and where to get help is **Alcoholics Anonymous,** simply known as **AA,** which is a rich source of simple informational pamphlets and literature on the topic as well as the location of **AA meetings** throughout the world. AA meeting locations and times can be found in local newspapers and are even held online. AA meetings use a 12 step recovery program to help alcoholics who want to stay sober. There are **open AA meetings** and **closed AA meetings.** Although closed meetings are for alcoholics only, **anyone interested in learning more about alcoholism is welcome to attend open meetings.** These meetings are one of the richest sources of information about alcoholism you will ever find. For additional information about Alcoholics Anonymous and other resources on alcoholism please refer to the **BIBLIOGRAPHY & RESOURCES** section of this book.

Another 12 step program associated with Alcoholics Anonymous is *Alanon*, a program for the spouses, family members and significant others affected by the alcoholic. *Alanon is a program for you.* By simply listening you will be surprised how much you learn.

1. You will learn that others have experienced the same problems and feelings that you have experienced.
2. You will learn what others tried that failed, and what works.
3. You will learn that you are not alone or unique.
4. You will learn that you need to take care of you, and how to do that.
5. You will learn that you have a support group to help you.
6. You will learn how to share the burden.
7. You will learn how to work the steps of Alanon.
8. You will learn about sponsorship and how a sponsor can help you.
9. You will learn how to set realistic limits.

Alcoholics Anonymous and Alanon are two of the best sources of information and help you will find on alcoholism, but these are not the only sources of information. *The internet* is a rich source of information and support. Of course you have to sort out the quality and accuracy of this information because you can get bad advice online as easily as you can get good advice. However, there are *other types of support groups* that are worthwhile, information about meeting times and locations as well as definitions and good information about the signs and symptoms of alcoholism. You may also have reached the point where you feel you could benefit from *counseling*. Chances are you know someone who is getting counseling who you can ask about who to see and where to go. The yellow pages of the *phone book* and your *personal physician* are also sources of information about where to find counseling in your community. Don't hesitate to get help you need; you are likely to find out a lot you didn't know that you need to know.

TIP # 3: LEARN WHAT TO EXPECT FROM THE ALCOHOLIC

As you begin to research alcoholism, talk to others who are supportive and attend meetings, the alcoholic in your life is likely to become quite uncomfortable. As anxiety builds the alcoholic will most likely try to convince you that you are overreacting and wasting your time because he has everything under control. If the alcoholic is successful in convincing you to back off, in a short period of time he is likely to resume his prior pattern of drinking behavior. If you do not appear convinced, the alcoholic may respond in a variety of ways depending on his personality and what he believes will work to get you stop focusing on the alcohol problem. *The alcoholic may even attempt to hold it together for a time* to convince you he really doesn't have a problem. Or, *he may resort to subterfuge* by sneaking around to drink and misleading you about where he is or what he is doing. *Another approach the alcoholic may try to use is to convince you that you are the problem.* He may tell you that you nag too much or that you aren't supportive enough and that he drinks because of stress caused by any number of sources outside of himself. The alcoholic has many tools at his disposal and he is not likely to give up his dependency on alcohol without a struggle.

Denial is one of the easiest and simplest defenses the alcoholic can use when asked whether he has a problem; if the alcoholic can convince self and others that he has no drinking problem, then logically there is no problem to address. A variation on denial that the alcoholic may use is to *minimize* the problem. When minimizing the alcoholic will paint his drinking as only an insignificant or small problem not worthy of the kind of scrutiny it is receiving. In minimizing he may make light of signs, symptoms or consequences of his drinking. ***Blame*** is another simple defense the alcoholic can use. For example, he may blame the boss for getting on him at work, giving him an excuse to have a few drinks after work to relax. Another example is when the alcoholic picks a fight with his wife and she takes the bait; he accuses her of nagging, which gives him the excuse he wants to go out to drink. Manipulation is another common defense the alcoholic is likely to use. ***Manipulation occurs when one says or does something designed to get another person to feel and act in a particular way***. The person using manipulation is playing a probability game; if I say this then you are likely to feel and act a particular way, based on your history. For example, if my wife tells me I haven't taken the trash out, then I am supposed to feel guilty and take the trash out. ***Managing*** is another tool the alcoholic uses to incorporate drinking as part of his lifestyle. He ***manages*** by arranging people and events to make it easier to maintain his drinking. For example, he may choose to associate with people he knows drink. He may arrange for leisure activities that involve drinking such as bowling, fishing trips, football parties or other activities that blend well with his drinking. By taking his wife to these activities, he may plan to mollify any complaints she may have. He may even choose a type of work, such as construction work, where his drinking appears to be more acceptable. Many of the alcoholic's defenses that I have described may already be familiar in one form or another to the person living with the alcoholic. Of course these defenses are only a sampling of responses available to the practicing alcoholic.

One of the more disturbing actions the alcoholic may take when his initial effort to get you to stop your quest for knowledge and support is intimidation. This ***intimidation may not only be verbal, but may take the form of physical abuse***. Such a response is most likely if there has been a history or pattern of abuse and/or if the alcoholic has been drinking. This response is dangerous for all parties concerned, including children present in the home. The appropriate response is to report the abuse to social services and to ***get help for yourself and other family members***. You will need to honestly cooperate with the abuse investigation. Even though this is difficult on several levels, ***it is essential to break a dangerous pattern than can result in emotional or physical harm or even death***. The investigation can result in positive outcomes. For example, it can become ***a powerful motivator for the alcoholic to get the help he needs*** to address his drinking problem and can provide for ongoing monitoring to insure compliance with a program for sobriety. The safety of family members is an immediate positive outcome. Therapy for family members ***may also lead to positive personal changes and adjustments in the family***. It is even possible for the recovering alcoholic to rejoin his healing family with continued support and supervision.

Of course it is possible that none of the negative defenses or outcomes I've described will occur. It is possible that the changes you have made and the actions you have taken may lead the alcoholic to use you as a frame of reference against which to compare his own behavior. In turn, ***the resulting anxiety may motivate the alcoholic to make an effort to make positive changes in his life***. If this happens consider yourself very fortunate. Based on my experience, it is important for you to identify your own limits and to develop your personal plan of action. You must be prepared not only for your own relapse, but for the alcoholic to relapse. Alcoholics often relapse several times before establishing a pattern of lasting sobriety. Next we will discuss how to identify your limits.

TIP # 4: IDENTIFY YOUR LIMITS & ACTIONS YOU WILL TAKE

What is a *limit*? For our purposes *a limit is that point where the status quo stops and change must occur*; in other words, it is like a figurative line in the sand. You may also notice that I have used the plural form of limit in the heading for this discussion. I did this because I believe, based on my experience, that many of us have several limits. Let's explore some examples. You may have a limit to how many excuses for drinking or episodes of drinking you will accept before you are willing to acknowledge that your spouse has a drinking problem. However, we may have to raise the bar higher for you to be willing to take the action step of seeking information or help. In other words, the limit for admitting a problem may be quite different from the limit for taking action to address the problem. Your limit for seeking information may be lower than the limit you set for getting help. The limit you set for getting help for yourself may be different than the limit you set for getting help for your spouse. We will address some questions to consider when identifying your limits and why it is important to identify limits.

It is common for the spouse of the alcoholic to want to believe and to trust the alcoholic. It is also common for the alcoholic to make numerous excuses to cover the drinking behavior. As the spouse you may even find yourself defending the alcoholic to friends, family members or the employer. How many excuses you accept or how much stress or pain you tolerate before taking some kind of action depends on your individual level of tolerance. *Is your limit when he forgets your anniversary, or your little girl's birthday party? Is your limit when he curses you and belittles you in front of the children or your friends? Is your limit when he gets fired for being drunk on the job? Is your limit when he goes to jail after injuring someone else in a drunken driving accident? Or, is your limit when he beats you up, or strikes one of the children? Is your limit when you catch him cheating on you?* These examples may seem extreme, but they are all too common occurrences in the lives of persons who live with practicing alcoholics. Although it may seem obvious, it is worth stating that it is important to identify your limits before you or someone you love is injured physically or emotionally. You, your children, the alcoholic and even members of the unsuspecting public can be at risk for injury or even death. If you are aware there is a problem but are struggling with your limits, what actions to take, or need more direction or support, it is time to consider a counselor. If you are reasonably certain that the problem centers around your spouse's alcohol abuse, you might want to see an alcohol counselor to help you sort out the problem and what actions to take.

What actions can you take? The first action you can take is one we've already visited – *learning everything you can about alcoholism.* You've already started the process by reading this book. If you follow through by attending Alanon and open AA meetings and reading AA pamphlets you will quickly gain the basic information you need. You may need the support and direction from your Alanon group and your counselor to decide what other steps to take and when. *Do you try to force the alcoholic into treatment? Do you stay in the relationship or leave? Do you get a job to pick up the financial slack? Do you get counseling for the children? Do you give him an ultimatum?* There are no easy answers to these questions. Of course *safety* is a primary consideration whenever there is significant risk of physical injury to the parties involved – namely you or your children. Your investment in the relationship is also a major consideration. If you have experienced several years of happy married life prior to the onset of the alcohol problem, you are probably going to be reluctant to give up on the relationship without a fight. However, it is important to understand that *alcoholism is progressive and is likely to worsen without intervention.* Your counselor can help you with intervention and/or referrals to other helping professionals if needed. Depending on the needs or problems, you or other family members may benefit from spiritual guidance, marital/family therapy, mental health services, or consultation with a physician or psychiatrist. ***In the following discussion you will find lists of unacceptable behaviors that the alcoholic may exhibit, and a list of practical "do's" and "don'ts" to consider as potential actions you can take***. Remember that any action you decide to take has consequences; inaction also has consequences. The key is to choose actions that are most likely to contribute to positive results for you and your family.

TIP # 5: BE AWARE OF POTENTIAL ALCOHOLIC BEHAVIORS

1. When questioned, the alcoholic is likely to deny or minimize his drinking behavior in an attempt to convince you that his drinking is normal and that you are mistaken.

2. When excuses and rationalizations fail to convince, the alcoholic is likely to blame you for his drinking and may even pick an argument as an excuse to drink.

3. A pattern of irresponsibility emerges characterized by failed promises, missed appointments, forgotten obligations and hallmark dates, coming home late and not showing up at work.

4. Verbal aggression is likely to increase towards you and your children in an attempt to intimidate, get you to feel responsible, or to get you to at least back off from identifying his drinking as a problem, or getting help for yourself and your children.

5. Over time aggression may escalate to physical assault towards you and the children.

6. More signs of his drinking problem start showing up outside the home, such as altercations with others, drunken driving, trouble at work, infidelity, etc.

TIP # 6: HERE ARE SOME PRACTICAL *DO'S* & *DON'TS* TO CONSIDER!

Do attend some open AA meetings and read the literature to learn the basics about alcoholism.

Do attend Alanon meetings to gain support and to learn more about how to cope with alcoholism in the family.

Do consider asking an experienced Alanon member you trust and respect to be your sponsor to help guide you.

Do seek out the help you need – be it from a substance abuse counselor, minister, mental health therapist, physician or other helping professional.

Do put safety first in the event you or your children are at risk and remove yourself to a safe place if warranted.

Do what you say you are going to do so the alcoholic and your children can trust that you mean what you say.

Do continue to learn, to seek help and support, and to take care of yourself and your children, including physical, safety, emotional, social and spiritual needs.

Don't nag. The alcoholic will learn to ignore you or, worse yet, use your nagging as an excuse to drink.

Don't make it easy for the alcoholic to drink by making excuses for him, bailing him out of jail, calling in sick for him, or by taking on his responsibilities or by minimizing the consequences of his drinking behaviors.

Don't make threats or give ultimatums you can't or won't follow through on.

Don't stay in a relationship that is unsafe!

Don't give up on yourself or your support system, regardless of whether or not you decide to stay in the relationship.

TIP # 7: YOU CAN TAKE STEPS TO HELP THE ALCOHOLIC GET PROPER HELP!

You have already started to help the alcoholic by learning about alcoholism and by getting help for yourself. These actions will serve as both a frame of reference and a motivator for the alcoholic to either attempt to make genuine changes, or to convince you he is making changes. If the attempt is real and not contrived, the alcoholic may be open to treatment options; you may want to begin by introducing him to a willing and experienced AA member. By this time you have probably identified such an individual through your attendance of open AA and Alanon meetings. An experienced AA member can introduce your alcoholic to the 12-step program, help him get started attending meetings, and suggest other treatment options such as outpatient therapy, if needed. All too often the preferred scenario doesn't work out and additional planning and action is needed.

If the alcoholic's continued alcohol consumption, relapse or other unacceptable behaviors show that he is either unable or unwilling to address his problem, it is time to consider other action steps. Consulting a reputable substance abuse counselor may be the next rational step to take. The counselor can help you sort out your feelings, clarify your perspective, and assess your resolve and the direction you want to take. Let's assume at this point you still want to salvage the relationship. The counselor can take the lead in helping plan an intervention. An intervention occurs with a planned event where family, friends and others familiar with the alcoholic's behavior meet with the alcoholic to confront the alcoholic with their feelings and observations related to his alcohol consumption. Prior to the actual intervention the counselor will meet with persons involved in the intervention to discuss the intervention, goals of the intervention, and to role play or rehearse what each person plans to say. It is usually the spouse who has the task of getting the alcoholic to be present at the location and time of the intervention. Of course the alcoholic is unaware of the real purpose of the appointment or who will be there. During the actual intervention the counselor directs the activity by encouraging the alcoholic to stay and hear what his friends and family have to say to him, and by calling on those present to take their turn sharing their feelings and observations. The object of the intervention is not to judge, but to help the alcoholic acknowledge his problem and to be willing to accept help. Of course the intervention may end in a number of ways.

If the intervention ends with the alcoholic's willingness to accept treatment, inpatient treatment may be a good choice. With the help of the counselor who planned the intervention, you should already have a reputable treatment program lined up and ready to accept your alcoholic. Inpatient treatment has several advantages. It separates the alcoholic from the environment and persons who enable or reinforce his drinking behaviors. It gives him time to become fully detoxed and to clear his head so he can look at his life without being immersed in everyday competing interests. He can also begin a treatment regimen without the competing negative outside environmental influences. The family may enjoy similar advantages during this time. The spouse can gain a clearer perspective free from the alcoholic's managing and manipulative behaviors. The spouse and children may enjoy a vacation from arguing or other aggressive behavior. After the alcoholic has begun to accept responsibility for his alcoholism and his recovery, treatment staff may opt to involve the family to attempt to reintegrate the alcoholic and to help the family understand what changes will take place and what recovery in their family will involve. This often involves some resentments and reluctance to accept the alcoholic back into family life. These feelings need to be addressed prior to discharging the alcoholic back into the home. Outpatient follow-up and 12-step meetings will be important for the alcoholic and the family during the ongoing post-discharge recovery process. Of course the intervention process doesn't always end with the alcoholic accepting treatment.

What if the alcoholic decides to walk out of the intervention? Suppose he blames his spouse and the others present and maintains he has no alcohol problem? Is the alcoholic a danger to self or others? If so, you may decide to file for emergency or involuntary commitment; it usually requires at least two people to file, and sometimes a statement from a clinical professional. A judge can issue an emergency order to have the individual in question evaluated. For involuntary commitment a hearing will be held and a judge will consider the evidence. If the alcoholic is found to be a danger to self or others, he may be ordered to undergo an evaluation and/or ordered to treatment, which may be inpatient or outpatient. What happens next?

The alcoholic who is forced into treatment by a court order may initially be angry and resistive, as well as covertly anxious and frightened. As the alcoholic is detoxified and bombarded with information, he may begin to respond to treatment over time. If treatment works, the alcoholic will commit to sobriety and an ongoing program of recovery. There is a myth that alcoholics who are coerced or forced into treatment will not benefit. That has not been my experience; of the thousands of substance abusers I worked with who entered treatment either on a voluntary basis or on a court order, outcomes were similar. Many individuals benefited from treatment, but some did not. *It is important to understand that admissions labeled as voluntary because there is no court order may be the result of coercion*. For example, the alcoholic may enter treatment because his boss told him to do so or lose his job. The wife may give her alcoholic husband an ultimatum to get treatment or the marriage is over. The alcoholic may enter treatment because he is too physically sick to function, or has lost his job or is homeless. *Few alcoholics wake up one fine morning and decide to check into treatment to self-actualize, or because it is the right thing to do; there is almost always a compelling motivator of some kind. It is even more important to understand it matters little how the alcoholic gets to treatment, but is vital how the alcoholic responds to treatment*. In my experience there are as many positive outcomes with coerced treatment as can be found with the true *voluntary* admission, which is in reality quite rare. As you read the literature, attend 12-step meetings, and talk with recovering alcoholics you will come to understand that *it usually requires multiple episodes of treatment with relapses intermingled before the alcoholic achieves lasting sobriety*. What if the alcoholic in your life docsn't achieve sobriety before you reach your tolerance limit?

TIP # 8: WHETHER YOU STICK IT OUT OR NOT, KEEP THE "ING" IN LIFE!

You've done your part to learn everything you can and to get help for yourself, your family and the alcoholic, yet the alcoholic has not taken the path to sobriety. You've reached your tolerance limit. You decide it is time to detach from the alcoholic, to let go of the codependent relationship with the alcoholic. This may be essential for your sanity and survival as well as for the health and welfare of children involved. The detachment may be a temporary separation until certain criteria are met. Such criteria may include treatment, sobriety, employment, no overt aggression, or other criteria that you have decided are essential to remaining in the relationship. Of course you may feel you have already exhausted all reasonable avenues and decide to seek divorce. Finally, there is always the option of remaining in the codependent relationship with the practicing alcoholic, in spite of the toxic effects on the entire family. So ... *what happens now*?

Regardless of whether you opt out of the relationship or decide to remain, continue your alanon meetings, practice what you've learned, use your support system, and continue counseling as needed for yourself and your children. If you stay in the relationship you will need the support in order to cope, and there is the possibility, however remote, that the alcoholic will eventually opt for sobriety. If you let go of the relationship grief is likely and you may need spiritual guidance or counseling for yourself and the family to adjust. You may find you also need to go to work and may need to see a vocational counselor for assistance. If divorce is in the picture, you will need an attorney to protect your interests, and the interests of your children. Of course this doesn't mean the end of the alcoholic! He is likely to be quite relentless in trying to get you to change your mind. You may be required to communicate with him because of your mutual interest in your children. In difficult cases, *a mediator may be required* to communicate between you and the alcoholic. *Don't despair; continue to actively care for yourself and your children. Life goes on!*

At first *you may feel lost and anxious about your new freedom and obligations.* When you are ready to do so, you can begin new relationships. As you adjust, you realize that your new beginning can start an exciting chapter in your life! *You will be able to set new goals and pursue activities you haven't experienced in years!* Life is not static. The world will not stand still because we have a few difficulties. It is important to *embrace life as a dynamic process. The "ing" in life is part of breathing, feeling, thinking, planning, behaving, working, playing and living.* It is my sincere hope that the tips in this book will help you help the alcoholic in your life, and, at the very least, help you in your continued journey through life. *Remember to keep the "ing" in your life!*

BIBLIOGRAPHY/RESOURCES

Alanon Family Group Headquarters. **Al-Anon's Twelve Steps & Traditions.** Virginia Beach, Virginia: Alanon Family Group Headquarters, Revised Edition, December 2005.

Alanon Family Groups. **How Alanon Works for Families & Friends of Alcoholics.** Virginia Beach, Virginia: Alanon Family Groups, 2008.

Beattie, Melody. **Codependent No More: How to Stop Controlling Others and Start Caring for Yourself.** Center City, Minnesota: Hazelden, 2nd Edition, September 1, 1986.

Bower, Sharon Anthony, and Gordon H. Bower. **Asserting Yourself: A Practical Guide for Positive Change.** Reading, Massachusetts: Addison-Wesley Publishing Company, 1991.

Ellis, Albert. **Feeling Better, Getting Better, Staying Better: Profound Self-Help Therapy for Your Emotions.** Atascadero, California: Impact Publishers, 2001.

Ellis, Keith. **The Magic Lamp: Goal Setting for People Who Hate Setting Goals.** New York: Three Rivers Press, 1998.

Kinney, Jean. **Loosening the Grip: A Handbook of Alcohol Information.** New York: McGraw-Hill, 10th Edition, April 12, 2011.

Leyden-Rubenstein, Lori A. **The Stress Management Handbook: Strategies for Health and Inner Peace.** Chicago, Illinois: Keats Publishing, 1999.

Maultsby, Maxie C. Jr., and Allie Hendricks. **You and Your Emotions.** Lexington, Kentucky: Rational Self-Help Books, 1974.

McHolland, James D. **Human Potential Seminar: Participant's Workbook.** Chicago: Kendall College Press, 1972.

Peale, Norman Vincent. **The Power of Positive Thinking.** New York: Touchstone First Fireside Edition, 2003.

Shenkle, Debra. **How to Self-Publish a Kindle Book: A Step-by-Step Guide.** Digital Edition. Amazon.com, 2012.

The Big Book On-line, Fourth Edition. Jefferson City, Missouri: Alcoholics Anonymous World Services, 2012. http://www.aa.org/bigbookonline/

ABOUT THE AUTHOR

Randy Young was born and raised in the Midwest region of the U.S.A. After high school the author worked a variety of jobs before getting married, having a family and pursuing his A.A., B.A., M.S. and Ph.D. degrees in the areas of human services, sociology, psychology, and training and learning. The author spent nearly 35 years working in the areas of mental health and substance abuse treatment. During this time Randy worked in nursing, social work, psychology and administration, and also enjoyed teaching as a college instructor. His primary life work has been dedicated to helping individuals learn to help themselves.

In his semi-retirement Randy has enjoyed spending time with his wife, children, grandchildren and friends while pursuing activities he loves such as camping, fishing, vacationing, reading and writing. During his years of employment Randy spent considerable time reading and writing in the capacity of his work for a professional clinical audience. Now it is the author's desire to apply his love of helping others and writing to a broader audience of readers.

Made in the USA
San Bernardino, CA
15 August 2018